Sports Illustrated KIDS

BEATING THE ODDS

THE GREATEST UPSETS IN SPORTS

by Thomas Kingsley Troupe

CAPSTONE PRESS
a capstone imprint

Published by Capstone Press, an imprint of Capstone
1710 Roe Crest Drive, North Mankato, Minnesota 56003
capstonepub.com

SPORTS ILLUSTRATED KIDS is a trademark of ABG-SI LLC.
Used with permission.

Library of Congress Cataloging-in-Publication Data
Names: Troupe, Thomas Kingsley, author.
Title: Beating the odds : the greatest upsets in sports / by Thomas
Kingsley Troupe.
Description: North Mankato, Minnesota : Capstone Press, [2023] |
Series: Sports illustrated kids. Heroes and heartbreakers | Includes
bibliographical references and index. | Audience: Ages 8-11 |
Audience: Grades 4-6 | Summary: "Underdog miracles, dynasty
defeats, and much more! In this Sports Illustrated Kids book, discover
the all-time greatest upsets in sports history. Read about the Celtics'
unbelievable win against the unstoppable Lakers in the 1969 NBA
Finals. Discover more about USA Hockey's miraculous defeat of
the Soviet Union at the 1980 Winter Olympics. And don't forget the
underdog Jets' remarkable win over the Colts in Super Bowl III. With
eye-popping photographs and heart-pounding text, this book will
turn any sports fan into a reading all-star!"— Provided by publisher.
Identifiers: LCCN 2022029344 (print) | LCCN 2022029345
(ebook) | ISBN 9781669011293 (hardcover) | ISBN 9781669011248
(paperback) | ISBN 9781669011255 (pdf) | ISBN 9781669011279
(kindle edition)
Subjects: LCSH: Sports upsets—Juvenile literature.
Classification: LCC GV705.4 .T75 2023 (print) | LCC GV705.4
(ebook) | DDC 796—dc23/eng/20220811
LC record available at https://lccn.loc.gov/2022029344
LC ebook record available at https://lccn.loc.gov/2022029345

Editorial Credits
Editor: Christianne Jones; Designer: Elyse White; Media Researcher:
Donna Metcalf; Production Specialist: Whitney Schaefer

Image and Design Element Credits
Alamy: PA Images, 7, Tribune Content Agency LLC, 19; Associated
Press: Andy Brownbill, 16, 17, AP Photo, 9, 13, 21, Ray Stubblebine,
20, Susan Ragan, 27 (bottom left); Getty Images: Jupiterimages, Brand
X Pictures, cover, LeArchitecto, cover (background), Tony Triolo,
25; Shutterstock: Annette Shaff, 28, Brocreative, 29, IYIKON, design
element (boxing icon), Oleksii Sidorov, 4, Palsur, design element
(icons), pambudi, design element (trophy icon), PHOTOCREO
Michal Bednarek, 5, Rauf Akhundof, design element (gymnastics
icon); Sports Illustrated: Erick W. Rasco, 11, Heinz Kluetmeier, 22,
Jerry Cooke, 23, Manny Millan, 27 (top right), SI Cover, 8, 15

All internet sites appearing in back matter were available and accurate
when this book was sent to press.

Printed and bound in the USA. PO# 5195

TABLE OF CONTENTS

Words in **bold** are in the glossary.

EXPECT THE UNEXPECTED

No one expected your football team to be in the championship. However, you've held your own the whole game. It's the end of the fourth quarter. The score is 21–19.

One kick decides if you'll be the champions. You run toward the ball and hope. Your foot connects with the football. The entire stadium gasps.

Throughout history, sports fans have learned that no team or athlete is indestructible. What seems like a one-sided match could turn around at any moment. No victory is ever guaranteed. Huddle up and relive some of the greatest upsets in sports history.

CHAPTER 1

DID THAT JUST HAPPEN?

Sports bring happiness, sadness, excitement, and moments of complete disbelief. Moments that don't seem possible become possible.

NO PROS, NO PROBLEM

In 2000, professional baseball players were allowed to compete in the Olympic Games. But because of the Major League Baseball (MLB) season schedule, the pro players weren't available.

FUN FACT

The 2000 Team USA was led by Hall of Fame MLB manager Tommy Lasorda. Before the 2000 Olympics, he had never before coached any of the players.

Team USA was made up of journeymen, minor leaguers, and lesser-known MLB players. They earned a spot in the finals against Cuba. Cuba won gold in the 1992 and 1996 Olympics. They were expected to win again.

In the first inning, Mike Neill hit a solo home run. Team USA's defense kept Cuba from scoring. In the fifth, Team USA scored three more runs. They shut out the Cubans 4–0 and brought home Olympic gold.

Team USA celebrates their win over Cuba.

THE GUARANTEE

During the 1968 football season, the New York Jets played well enough to land in Super Bowl III. They would face the Baltimore Colts. Led by famed quarterback Johnny Unitas, the Colts were favored by many to destroy the Jets.

Three days before the game, Jets quarterback Joe Namath told reporters, "We're gonna win the game. I guarantee it."

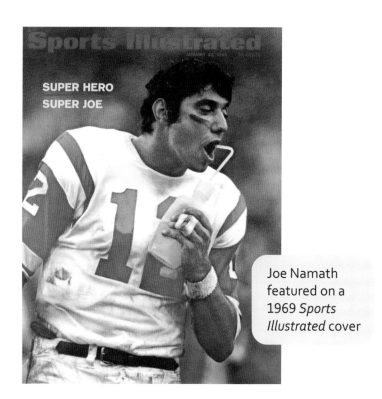

Joe Namath featured on a 1969 *Sports Illustrated* cover

Namath getting ready to hand off the ball

The Colts came on strong. But Namath fired short passes and moved the Jets down the field. By the fourth quarter, the Jets had a 16–0 lead. The Colts finally scored a touchdown and an extra point, but it wasn't enough.

On January 12, 1969, Namath delivered on his guarantee. The Jets shocked the world and beat the Colts 16–7 for the championship.

CHAPTER 2
WHEN THE MIGHTY FALL

The number-one player does not always win. That's why the game is played. Even the best can lose.

THE UNDERDOG

Naomi Osaka faced her tennis idol, Serena Williams, in the 2018 U.S. Open. Just 20 years old, Osaka was the underdog. Williams was hoping for her 24th Grand Slam trophy. No one expected what happened that day. Osaka outplayed Williams. She served better and made fewer mistakes, beating Williams and winning the first set.

FUN FACT

A Grand Slam in professional tennis is winning all four major championships—Australian Open, French Open, Wimbledon, and the U.S. Open—in the same calendar year.

Williams (front) and Osaka pose together before the big match.

Williams came back in the first half of the second set until she returned a ball into the net. She became frustrated and broke her racket in anger. After outbursts with the line judges, Williams was done. Osaka beat the champion 6–2, 6–4 and won her first Grand Slam Title.

THE GREATEST VS. THE LATEST

In 1978, Muhammad Ali was one of the greatest boxers of all time. Leon Spinks was an Olympic gold medal boxer who had fought professionally only seven times.

On February 15, 1978, the two came face-to-face in a ring in Las Vegas, Nevada. Ali looked like he was barely trying in the first few rounds. Spinks built an early lead. Seeing his title slipping away, Ali tried to knock out Spinks. Spinks fought back. It was a fight no one expected to see, and before long, it was over.

After 15 brutal rounds, the judges crowned Spinks the new champion. After the fight, Spinks said about Ali, "He's still the greatest; I'm just the latest."

FUN FACT

The official name of boxing is actually pugilism, which means "practice and skills of fighting with fists."

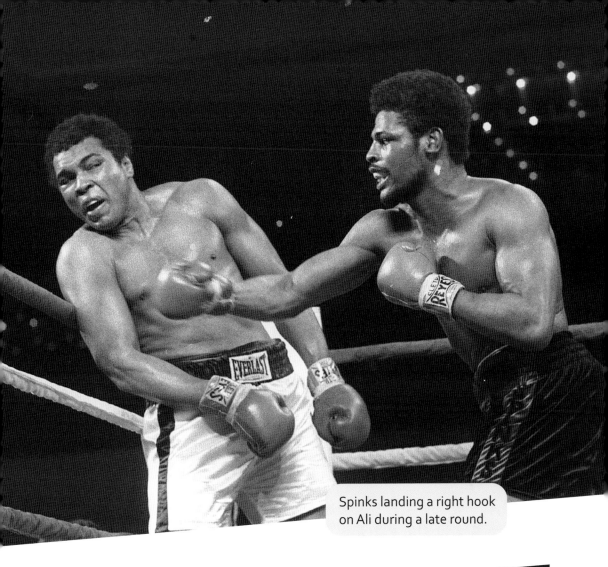

Spinks landing a right hook on Ali during a late round.

SIDEBAR

Though Ali lost to Spinks in 1978, the two fought again seven months later. Ali beat Spinks in the rematch and won the heavyweight title for the third time. Spinks kept fighting after the loss, but never wore the championship belt again.

CHAPTER 3
ALMOST PERFECT

Having a perfect record or a perfect game is a dream. It's not easy to do, which is why it doesn't happen very often.

ONE AWAY FROM PERFECT

In 2007, the New England Patriots were having an amazing football season. Led by quarterback Tom Brady, the Patriots won all of their regular-season games. Winning the Super Bowl meant the Patriots would have a perfect season. The New York Giants had other plans.

FUN FACT

The only NFL team to achieve a "perfect season" was the Miami Dolphins in 1972.

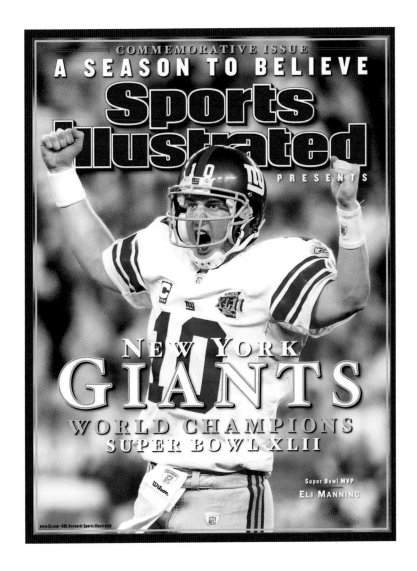

On February 3, 2008, Giants quarterback Eli Manning threw the game-winning touchdown with 35 seconds left in the fourth quarter. The Giants won the Super Bowl with a score of 17–14. They snatched away the Patriots dream of a truly perfect season.

A KICK TO THE HEAD

Mixed Martial Arts (MMA) is a brutal sport. It pits two fighters in an eight-sided cage called an Octagon. Kicks and punches fly until one fighter is named the winner. In the world of women's MMA, no one was as unstoppable as Ronda Rousey.

Holly Holm was expected to be another in a string of fighters Rousey knocked out. A former boxing champ, Holm had never even finished an Ultimate Fighting Championship (UFC) fight. On November 14, 2015, all that changed.

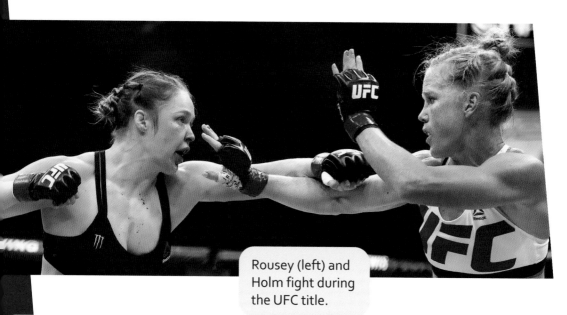

Rousey (left) and Holm fight during the UFC title.

Holm holding the champion belt after her big win

In the first round, Holm hit Rousey and stunned the champion. She grappled and took Rousey down. Rousey got up and chased Holm around the ring, throwing sloppy punches. In the second round, Holm caught Rousey with a kick to the head, knocking the champ down. Rousey's undefeated record was over.

CHAPTER 4

UNBELIEVABLE!

Nothing is more exciting than the last-second play. The sports miracle! The moment nobody will forget.

BUZZER-BEATER

During the 1989 NBA Eastern Conference first round, the Cleveland Cavaliers and Bulls traded wins. In the fifth and deciding game, the Cavaliers were ahead 100–99. With three seconds left in the game, the Bulls called a time-out. They needed a miracle.

FUN FACT

Michael Jordan planned on becoming a TV meteorologist if his career in basketball didn't go well.

Jordan celebrating after his game-winning basket

With the ball back in play, Jordan got the pass. As the final seconds ticked away, he jumped and fired. The ball tapped the rim and dropped through the hoop. The Bulls won with what became known as "The Shot"—Jordan's famous buzzer-beater.

WIN WHEN IT MATTERS

Despite many regular-season losses during the 1973 MLB season, the New York Mets found themselves in the National League Championship Series. They faced the Cincinnati Reds, known then as the "Big Red Machine."

Jerry Koosman pitching in game 3 of the playoffs

Willie Mays drives in a run during the fifth inning in Game 5

The final game in the series saw the Mets pull out all the stops. After a tie game in the fourth inning, the Mets scored four runs in the fifth inning. Then they continued to put runs up on the board. The Big Red Machine had run out of gas. The Mets won the game 7–2. They won the NL pennant with the lowest win percentage in MLB history.

MIRACLE ON ICE

The Soviet Union, which included Russia and a number of smaller countries, dominated Olympic hockey. For four Winter Games in a row, they took home gold medals. So when U.S. college hockey players were called to compete in the 1980 Olympic Games, no one expected many wins.

The two undefeated teams faced off on February 22, 1980. The Soviets played strong, outshooting the Americans. After about nine minutes into the third period, Team USA tied the game at 3–3. With 10 minutes left to play, the U.S. fired a 25-foot (7.6-meter) wrist shot past the Soviet goalie. For the first time, Team USA was ahead.

Dave Christian launches a wrist shot against the Soviet Union.

Mike Ramsey (right) defends a Soviet Player.

After that goal, the Americans held strong and won, 4–3. Many people believe it is the biggest upset in sports history.

SIDEBAR

Defeating the Soviet Union didn't automatically guarantee Team USA gold. The Americans advanced to face Finland and beat them 4–2, earning them their well-deserved Olympic gold medal.

CHAPTER 5

IT'S NOT OVER 'TIL IT'S OVER

The clock reads zero. The game is over. There is a winner and a loser. But sometimes the game still isn't done.

JUST TWO POINTS

By 1969, the Boston Celtics had won 10 basketball championships. But the players were getting older, and injuries bothered some of them. Still, they were headed to the NBA Finals. This time they were playing the Los Angeles Lakers.

FUN FACT

The Los Angeles Lakers and the Boston Celtics are tied for the most NBA Championships with 17 each.

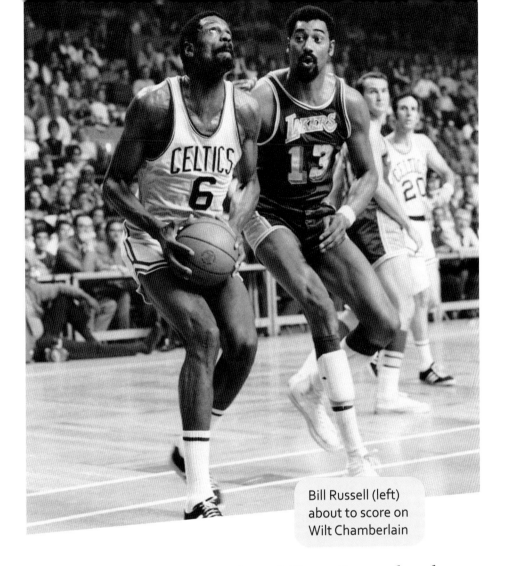

Bill Russell (left) about to score on Wilt Chamberlain

The series was tied, and Game 7 was played in Los Angeles. With the home court advantage, the Lakers were sure they would win. They even had balloons waiting in the rafters to drop onto the court. The balloons never fell that night, as the Celtics squeaked by in a close victory, beating the Lakers 108–106.

NO PAIN, NO GAIN

Winning Olympic gold medals in women's gymnastics was something Russia excelled at. The United States hoped to change that at the 1996 Summer Olympics in Atlanta, Georgia. The United States formed a team of women gymnasts known as the Magnificent Seven.

The Americans had a solid lead going into the last event, which was the vault. Two U.S. gymnasts were ready to compete. Dominique Moceanu went first. She had two rough landings. Last up was Kerri Strug. On her first attempt, Strug landed hard, twisting her ankle. Limping, she asked coach Béla Károlyi, "Do we need this?" The answer was yes.

FUN FACT

Before the 1996 Olympics, the Russian women's team had won gold in 10 consecutive Olympic Games.

Strug (above) after her second vault, and being carried by her coach (left) after the award ceremony

In intense pain, Strug ran to the vault. She hit the springboard, flipped through the air, and landed clean on one foot. Her score? 9.712, enough to clinch the gold for the Magnificent Seven.

BACK TO THE BEGINNING

You watch the football flip end-over-end as it arcs its way toward the goal posts. The stands, packed with fans of the other team, watch in horror. Everyone doubted your team would even get here. There's no doubt that the kick is good as it sails through the uprights. The underdogs have won! What an upset!

Sports are a physical and mental challenge. Having the mindset that a win is impossible is the first step to defeat. As the world has shown time and time again, no triumph is a sure thing. Great upsets are what makes sports worth playing and watching!

GLOSSARY

consecutive
(kuhn-SEK-yuh-tiv)
when something
happens several times in
a row without a break

excel (ik-SEL)
to be superior in a
certain area

idol (EYE-duhl)
someone who is
worshipped

journeyman
(JUR-nee-muhn)
a player who has played
for a number of different
teams

undefeated
(uhn-dih-FEET-id)
never lost

underdog
(UHN-der-dawg)
a person or team that is
not expected to win an
event

READ MORE

Abdo, Kenny. *Miracle Moments in Football.* Minneapolis: Abdo Zoom, 2022.

Marthaler, Jon. *Bad Days in Sports.* North Mankato, MN: Capstone Publishing, 2017.

Seidel, Jeff. *Pro Baseball Upsets.* Minneapolis: Lerner Publishing, 2020.

INTERNET SITES

Greatest Upsets in Sports History
sikids.com/si-kids/greatest-upsets-sports-history

List of Kids Sports
rookieroad.com/sports/kids-sports-list

Time for Kids: Sports
timeforkids.com/g56/topics/sports

INDEX

ABOUT THE AUTHOR

Thomas Kingsley Troupe is the author of a big ol' pile of books for kids. He's written about everything from ghosts to Bigfoot to third-grade werewolves. He even wrote a book about dirt. When he's not writing or reading, he investigates the strange and spooky as part of the Twin Cities Paranormal Society. Thomas lives in Woodbury, Minnesota, with his two sons.